FIFTY DAYS WITH JESUS

JOURNALING THROUGH THE GOSPEL OF MARK

First Alhambra Methodist

Craig Kennet Miller

About the Author

The Rev. Dr. Craig Kennet Miller is the English Ministry Pastor at First Alhambra Methodist Church in Alhambra, California. The former Director of Congregational Development at Discipleship Ministries, he is the author of numerous books including *Boomer Spirituality: Seven Values for the Second Half of Life* and *iKids: Parenting in the Digital Age*. His journal books include *The Story of Christmas* and *The Angels Sang*.

Fifty Days with Jesus is available at www.amazon.com.

All royalties support the ministry of Alhambra First United Methodist Church.

Fifty Days with Jesus: Journaling through the Gospel of Mark © 2021 by Alhambra First UMC. All rights reserved. Printed in the United States of America.

Scripture readings are from the Open English Bible. The OEB is under a Creative Commons Zero license and in the public domain. People may quote or copy scriptures verses without restrictions. www.openenglishbible.org.

© 2021 Craig Kennet Miller, Alhambra First United Methodist Church. 9 N. Almansor St., Alhambra, CA, 91801

ISBN 9798598083833

INTRODUCTION

Have you ever wanted to read a firsthand account of the life of Jesus? Fifty Days with Jesus: Journaling through the Gospel of Mark gives you an opportunity to immerse yourself in the ministry of Jesus, as you devote yourself to daily readings, reflection, and prayer over the next seven weeks.

In this journal, you will read through the Gospel of Mark, followed by readings from John, Luke, and Acts. This will give you a full picture of Jesus' ministry from his baptism by John the Baptist to his resurrection appearances to his disciples.

The Gospel of Mark is the earliest recorded history of the life of Jesus. As the first Gospel, both Matthew and Luke were based on this early account of the ministry of Jesus.

Most scholars identify the writer as being John Mark, a close companion of the Apostle Peter. As a fellow traveler with Peter, he had firsthand access to the stories of Jesus. His account is so trustworthy, almost 90% of Matthew has a direct link to Mark. Mark was probably written around 64 AD, a little over 30 years after the death and resurrection of Jesus.

As you journal through Mark, you will be invited to identify three words or phrases that speak to you from the scripture of the day. By interacting with the stories of Jesus, you will have a more in-depth experience. Also, you will be invited to write down your prayers for the day.

Fifty Days with Jesus can be used for a church-wide experience. The readings start on a Sunday and finish on a Sunday, making it perfect for an eight-week Sunday study, sermon series, or for the Lenten Season.

As you immerse yourself the Gospel of Mark, I hope you hear the powerful message of salvation and grace found in Jesus Christ.

Blessings.

Craig Kennet Miller

TABLE OF CONTENTS

50 DAYS WITH JESUS ON YOUTUBE

Starting Sunday, February 21st, 2021, you can watch and listen to daily readings of the scripture of the day. This will continue through Easter on April 4th, and finish on Sunday, April 11th. Also, be sure to join us for worship on Sundays at the First Alhambra Methodist YouTube Channel.

Go to www.youtube.com

In the search bar type: First Alhambra Methodist

Go to the 50 Days with Jesus Playlist or watch on

the First Alhambra Methodist Channel

.

WEEK ONE

THE ONE

MARK 1:1 - 2:28

DAY 1   MARK 1:1-13   SUNDAY

The beginning of the good news about Jesus Christ. It is said in the prophet Isaiah – 'I am sending my messenger ahead of you; he will prepare your way.

The voice of one crying aloud in the wilderness: "Prepare the road for the Lord, make a straight path for him."'

John the Baptizer appeared in the wilderness, proclaiming a baptism on repentance, for the forgiveness of sins. The whole of Judea, as well as all the inhabitants of Jerusalem, went out to him; and they were baptized by him in the Jordan River, confessing their sins. John wore clothes made of camels' hair, with a leather strap around his waist, and lived on locusts and wild honey; and he proclaimed – "After me is coming someone more powerful than I am, and I am not fit even to stoop down and unfasten his sandals. I have baptized you with water, but he will baptize you with the Holy Spirit."

Now about that time Jesus came from Nazareth in Galilee, and was baptized by John in the Jordan. Just as he was coming up out of the water, he saw the heavens split open and the Spirit coming down to him like a dove, and from the heavens came a voice – "You are my dearly loved son; you bring me great joy."

Immediately afterward the Spirit drove Jesus out into the wilderness; and he was there in the wilderness forty days, tempted by Satan, and among the wild beasts, while the angels helped him.

REFLECTION

Write down three words or phrases from this passage:

1.

2.

3.

What does this say about Jesus?

My Prayers for Today

For myself:

For my family and friends:

For my church and community:

For our World:

Other:

DAY 2   MARK 1:14-20   MONDAY

After John had been arrested, Jesus went to Galilee, proclaiming the good news of God – "The time has come, and the kingdom of God is at hand; repent, and believe the good news." As Jesus was going along the shore of the Sea of Galilee, he saw Simon and his brother Andrew casting a net in the sea, for they were fishermen. "Come and follow me," Jesus said, "and I will teach you to fish for people." They left their nets at once, and followed him. Going on a little further, he saw James, Zebedee's son, and his brother John, who were in their boat mending the nets. Jesus called them at once, and they left their father Zebedee in the boat with the crew, and went after him.

11

REFLECTION

Write down three words or phrases from this passage:

1.

2.

3.

What does this say about Jesus?

My Prayers for Today

For myself:

For my family and friends:

For my church and community:

For our World:

Other:

DAY 3   MARK 1:21-34   TUESDAY

They walked to Capernaum. On the next Sabbath Jesus went into the synagogue and began to teach. The people were amazed at his teaching, for he taught them like one who had authority, and not like the teachers of the Law. Now there was in their synagogue at the time a man under the power of a foul spirit, who called out, "What do you want with us, Jesus the Nazarene? Have you come to destroy us? I know who you are – the Holy One of God!" But Jesus rebuked the spirit, "Be silent! Come out from him." The foul spirit threw the man into a fit, and with a loud cry came out from him. They were all so amazed that they kept asking each other, "What is this? What is this, a new kind of teaching? He gives his commands with authority even to the foul spirits, and they obey him!" His fame spread at once in all directions, through the whole region of Galilee. As soon as they had left the synagogue, they went to the house of Simon and Andrew, along with James and John. Now Simon's mother-in-law was lying ill with a fever, and they at once told Jesus about her. Jesus went up to her and, grasping her hand, raised her up; the fever left her, and she began to take care of them. In the evening, after sunset, the people brought to Jesus all who were ill or possessed by demons; and the whole city was gathered around the door. Jesus cured many who were ill with various diseases, and drove out many demons, and would not permit them to speak, because they knew him to be the Christ.

REFLECTION

Write down three words or phrases from this passage:

1.

2.

3.

What does this say about Jesus?

My Prayers for Today

For myself:

For my family and friends:

For my church and community:

For our World:

Other:

DAY 4   MARK 1:35-45   WEDNESDAY

In the morning, long before daylight, Jesus got up and went out to a lonely spot, and there he began to pray. But Simon and his companions went out searching for him; and, when they found him, they exclaimed, "Everyone is looking for you!" But Jesus said to them, "Let us go somewhere else, into the country towns nearby so that I can make my proclamation in them also; for that was why I came." And he went about making his proclamation in their synagogues all through Galilee, and driving out the demons.

One day a leper came to Jesus and, falling on his knees, begged him for help. "If only you are willing," he said, "you are able to make me clean." Moved with compassion, Jesus stretched out his hand and touched him, saying as he did so, "I am willing; become clean." Instantly the leprosy left the man, and he became clean; and then Jesus, after sternly warning him, immediately sent him away, and said to him, "Be careful not to say anything to anyone; but go and show yourself to the priest, and make the offerings for your cleansing directed by Moses, as evidence of your cure." The man, however, went away, and began to speak about it publicly, and to spread the story so widely, that Jesus could no longer go openly into a town, but stayed outside in lonely places; and people came to him from every direction.

REFLECTION

Write down three words or phrases from this passage:

1.

2.

3.

What does this say about Jesus?

My Prayers for Today

For myself:

For my family and friends:

For my church and community:

For our World:

Other:

DAY 5   MARK 2:1-11   THURSDAY

Some days later, when Jesus came back to Capernaum, the news spread that he was in a house there; and so many people collected together, that after a while there was no room for them even around the door; and he began to tell them his message. Some people came, bringing to him a paralyzed man, who was being carried by four of them. Being, however, unable to get him near to Jesus, owing to the crowd, they removed the roofing above Jesus; and, when they had made an opening, they let down the mat on which the paralyzed man was lying. When Jesus saw their faith, he said to the man, "Child, your sins are forgiven."

But some of the teachers of the Law who were sitting there were debating in their minds, "Why does this man speak like this? He is blaspheming! Who can forgive sins except God?" Jesus, at once intuitively aware that they were debating with themselves in this way, said to them, "Why are you debating in your minds about this? Which is easier? – to say to the paralyzed man, 'Your sins are forgiven'? Or to say 'Get up, and take up your mat, and walk'? But so you may know that the Son of Man has power to forgive sins on earth" – here he said to the paralyzed man – "To you I say, Get up, take up your mat, and return to your home." The man got up, and immediately took up his mat, and went out before them all; at which they were amazed, and, as they praised God, they said, "We have never seen anything like this!"

REFLECTION

Write down three words or phrases from this passage:

1.

2.

3.

What does this say about Jesus?

My Prayers for Today

For myself:

For my family and friends:

For my church and community:

For our World:

Other:

DAY 6   MARK 2:12-17   FRIDAY

Jesus went out again to the sea; and all the people came to him, and he taught them. As he went along, he saw Levi, the son of Alphaeus, sitting in the tax office, and said to him, "Follow me." Levi got up and followed him.

Later on he was in his house having dinner, and a number of tax-gatherers and outcasts took their places at the table with Jesus and his disciples; for many of them were following him. When the teachers of the Law belonging to the party of the Pharisees saw that he was eating in the company of such people, they said to his disciples, "Why does he eat with the tax-gatherers and outcasts?"

Hearing this, Jesus said, "It is not those who are healthy who need a doctor, but those who are ill. I did not come to call the religious, but the outcast."

REFLECTION

Write down three words or phrases from this passage:

1.

2.

3.

What does this say about Jesus?

My Prayers for Today

For myself:

For my family and friends:

For my church and community:

For our World:

Other:

DAY 7   MARK 2:18-27   SATURDAY

Now John's disciples and the Pharisees were fasting, and people came and asked Jesus, "Why is it that John's disciples and the disciples of the Pharisees fast, while yours do not?" Jesus answered, "Can the groom's friends fast, while the groom is with them? As long as they have the groom with them, they cannot fast. But the days will come, when the groom will be taken away from them, and they will fast then – when that day comes."

"No one ever sews a piece of unshrunk cloth on an old garment; if they do, the patch tears away from it – the new from the old – and a worse tear is made. And no one ever puts new wine into old wine-skins; if they do, the wine will burst the skins, and both the wine and the skins are lost. But new wine is put into fresh skins."

One Sabbath, as Jesus was walking through the cornfields, his disciples began to pick the ears of wheat as they went along. "Look!" the Pharisees said to him, "why are they doing what is not allowed on the Sabbath?"

"Have you never read," answered Jesus, "what David did when he was in need and hungry, he and his companions – how he went into the house of God, in the time of Abiathar the high priest, and ate the consecrated bread, which only the priests are allowed to eat, and gave some to his comrades as well?"

Then Jesus added, "The Sabbath was made for people, and not people for the Sabbath; so the Son of Man is lord even of the Sabbath."

REFLECTION

Write down three words or phrases from this passage:

1.

2.

3.

What does this say about Jesus?

My Prayers for Today

For myself:

For my family and friends:

For my church and community:

For our World:

Other:

WEEK TWO

THE HEALER

MARK 3:1 - 5:43

DAY 8   MARK 3:1-12   SUNDAY

On another occasion Jesus went in to a synagogue, where there was a man whose hand was withered. And they watched Jesus closely, to see if he would cure the man on the Sabbath, so that they might have a charge to bring against him. "Stand out in the middle," Jesus said to the man with the withered hand; and to the people he said, "Is it allowable to do good at the Sabbath – or harm? To save a life, or destroy it?" As they remained silent, Jesus looked around at them in anger, grieving at the hardness of their hearts, and said to the man, "Stretch out your hand." The man stretched it out; and his hand had become   sound. Immediately   on leaving the synagogue, the Pharisees and the Herodians united in laying a plot against Jesus, to put him to death.

Then Jesus went away with his disciples to the sea, followed by a great number of people from Galilee. A great number, hearing of all that he was doing, came to him from Judea, from Jerusalem, from Edom, from beyond the Jordan, and from the country around Tyre and Sidon. So Jesus told his disciples to keep a small boat close by, so that the crowd would not crush him. For he had cured many of them, and so people kept crowding around him, so all who were sick might touch him. The foul spirits, too, whenever they caught sight of him, flung themselves down before him, and screamed out, "You are the Son of God"! But he repeatedly warned them not to make him known.

REFLECTION

Write down three words or phrases from this passage:

1.

2.

3.

What does this say about Jesus?

My Prayers for Today

For myself:

For my family and friends:

For my church and community:

For our World:

Other:

DAY 9   MARK 3:13-35   MONDAY

Jesus made his way up the hill, and called those whom he wished; and they went to him. He appointed twelve – whom he also named 'apostles' – so that they might be with him, and that he might send them out as his messengers, to preach, and with power to drive out demons. So he appointed the Twelve – Peter (which was the name that Jesus gave to Simon), James, the son of Zebedee, and his brother John (to whom he gave the name of Boanerges, which means the Thunderers), Andrew, Philip, Bartholomew, Matthew, Thomas, James the son of Alphaeus, Thaddaeus, Simon the Zealot, and Judas Iscariot, the man who betrayed him.

Jesus went into a house; and again a crowd collected, so that they were not even able to eat their food. When his relatives heard of it, they went to take charge of him, for they said that he was out of his mind.

The teachers of the Law, who had come down from Jerusalem, said, "He has Beelzebul in him! He drives the demons out by the help of their chief." So Jesus called them to him, and answered them in parables, "How can Satan drive out Satan? When a kingdom is divided against itself, it cannot last; and when a household is divided against itself, it will not be able to last. So, if Satan is in revolt against himself and is divided, he cannot last – his end has come!

"No man who has broken into a strong man's house can carry off his goods, without first tying him up; and not until then will he plunder his house. I tell you that people will be forgiven everything – their sins, and all the slanders that they utter; but whoever slanders the Holy Spirit remains unforgiven to the end; he has to answer for an enduring sin." This was said in reply to the charge that he had a foul spirit in him. His mother and his brothers came, and stood outside, and sent to ask him to come to them. There was a crowd sitting around Jesus, and some of them said to him, "Look, your mother and your brothers are outside, asking for you."

"Who is my mother? And my brothers?" was his reply. Then he looked around on the people sitting in a circle around him, and said, "Here are my mother and my brothers! Whoever does the will of God is my brother and sister and mother.

REFLECTION	My Prayers for Today
Write down three words or phrases from this passage:	For myself:
	For my family and friends:
1.	
2.	For my church and community:
3.	
What does this say about Jesus?	For our World:
	Other:

DAY 10   MARK 4:1-20   TUESDAY

Jesus again began to teach by the sea; and, as an immense crowd was gathering around him, he got into a boat, and sat in it on the sea, while all the people were on the shore at the water's edge.

Then he taught them many truths in parables; and in the course of his teaching he said to them:

"Listen! The sower went out to sow; and presently, as he was sowing, some of the seed fell along the path; and the birds came, and ate it up. Some fell on rocky ground, where it had not much soil, and, because the soil wasn't deep, sprang up at once; but, when the sun rose, it was scorched, and, because their roots were not deep enough, withered away. Some of the seed fell among brambles; but the brambles shot up and completely choked it, and it yielded no return. Some fell into good soil, and, shooting up and growing, yielded a return, amounting to thirty, sixty, and even a hundred fold." And Jesus said, "Let anyone who has ears to hear with hear."

Afterward, when he was alone, his followers and the Twelve asked him about his parables; and he said, "To you the hidden truth of the kingdom of God has been imparted; but to those who are outside it all teaching takes the form of parables so that – 'Though they have eyes, they may see without perceiving; and though they have ears, they may hear without understanding; otherwise some day they might turn and be forgiven.'"

"You do not know the meaning of this parable?" he went on, "Then how will you understand all the other parables? The sower sows the message. The people meant by the seed that falls along the path are these – where the message is sown, but, as soon as they have heard it, Satan immediately comes and carries away the message that has been sown in them. So, too, those meant by the seed sown on the rocky places are the people who, when they have heard the message, at once accept it joyfully; but, as they have no root, they stand only for a short time; and so, when trouble or persecution arises because of the message, they fall away at once. Those meant by the seed

sown among the brambles are different; they are the people who hear the message, but the cares of life, and the glamour of wealth, and cravings for many other things come in and completely choke the message, so that it gives no return. But the people meant by the seed sown on the good ground are those who hear the message, and welcome it, and yield a return, thirty, sixty, and even a hundred fold."

REFLECTION	My Prayers for Today
Write down three words or phrases from this passage:	For myself:
	For my family and friends:
1.	
2.	
3.	For my church and community:
What does this say about Jesus?	For our World
	Other:

DAY 11   MARK 4:21-34   WEDNESDAY

Jesus said to them, "Is a lamp brought to be put under a basket or under the couch, instead of being put on the lamp-stand? There is nothing hidden that will not come to light and nothing is concealed that will not be brought into the open. Let all who have ears to hear with hear.

"Take care what you listen to," said Jesus. "The standard you use will be used for you, and more will be added for you. For, to those who have, more will be given; while, from those who have nothing, even what they have will be taken away."

Jesus also said, "This is what the kingdom of God is like – like a man who has scattered seed on the ground, and then sleeps by night and rises by day, while the seed is shooting up and growing – he knows not how. The ground bears the crop

of itself – first the blade, then the ear, and then the full grain in the ear; but,

as soon as the crop is ready, immediately he puts in the sickle because harvest has come."

Jesus also said, "To what can we liken the kingdom of God? By what can we illustrate it? Perhaps by the growth of a mustard seed. This seed, when sown in the ground, though it is smaller than all other seeds, yet, when sown, shoots up, and becomes larger than any other herb, and puts out great branches, so that even the wild birds can roost in its shelter."

With many such parables Jesus used to speak to the people of his message, as far as they were able to receive it; and to them he never used to speak except in parables; but in private to his own disciples he explained everything.

REFLECTION

Write down three words or phrases from this passage:

1.

2.

3.

What does this say about Jesus?

My Prayers for Today

For myself:

For my family and friends:

For my church and community:

For our World:

Other:

DAY 12   MARK 4:35-5:13   THURSDAY

In the evening of the same day, Jesus said to them, "Let us go across." So, leaving the crowd behind, they took him with them, just as he was, in the boat; and there were other boats with him. A violent squall came on, and the waves kept dashing into the boat, so that the boat was actually filling. Jesus was in the stern asleep on the cushion; and the disciples roused him and cried, "Teacher! Is it nothing to you that we are lost?" Jesus rose and rebuked the wind, and said to the sea, "Hush! Be still!" Then the wind dropped, and a great calm followed. "Why are you so timid?" he exclaimed. "Have you no faith yet?" But they were struck with great awe, and said to one another, "Who can this be that even the wind and the sea obey him?"

They came to the other side of the sea – the region of the Gerasenes; and, as soon as Jesus had got out of the boat, he met a man coming out of the tombs, who was under the power of a foul spirit, and who made his home in the tombs. No one had ever been able to secure him, even with a chain; for, though he had many times been left secured with fetters and chains, he had snapped the chains and broken the fetters to pieces, and no one could master him. Night and day alike, he was continually shrieking in the tombs and among the hills, and cutting himself with stones. Catching sight of Jesus from a distance, he ran and bowed to the ground before him, shrieking out in a loud voice, "What do you want with me, Jesus, Son of the Most High God? For God's sake do not torment me!" For Jesus had said, "Come out from the man, you foul spirit." And he asked him, "What is your name?" "My name," he said, "is Legion, for there are many of us;" and he begged Jesus again and again not to send them away out of that country.

There was a large drove of pigs close by, feeding on the hillside; and the spirits begged Jesus, "Send us into the pigs so that we can take possession of them." Jesus gave them leave. They came out, and entered into the pigs; and the drove – about two thousand in number – rushed down the steep slope into the sea and were drowned in the sea.

REFLECTION	My Prayers for Today
Write down three words or phrases from this passage:	For myself:
	For my family and friends:
1.	For my church and community:
2.	
3.	For our World
What does this say about Jesus?	Other:

DAY 13 MARK 5:14-24 FRIDAY

Then the men who tended them ran away, and carried the news to the town, and to the country around; and the people went to see what had happened. When they came to Jesus, they found the possessed man sitting there, clothed and in his right mind – the man who had had the 'Legion' in him – and they were awe-struck. Then those who had seen it related to them all that had happened to the possessed man, as well as about the pigs; so they began to beg Jesus to leave their region.

As Jesus was getting into the boat, the possessed man begged him to let him stay with him. But Jesus refused. "Go back to your home, to your own people," he said, "and tell them of all that the Lord has done for you, and how he took pity on you." So the man went, and began to proclaim in the district of the Ten Towns all that Jesus had done for him; and everyone was amazed.

By the time Jesus had recrossed in the boat to the opposite shore, a great number of people had gathered to meet him, and were standing by the sea. One of the leaders of the synagogue, whose name was Jairus, came and, as soon as he saw Jesus, threw himself at his feet and begged him repeatedly, saying, "My little daughter is at death's door. Please come and place your hands on her so that she may recover and live." So Jesus went with him. A great number of people followed Jesus, and kept pressing around him.

REFLECTION

Write down three words or phrases from this passage:

1.

2.

3.

What does this say about Jesus?

My Prayers for Today

For myself:

For my family and friends:

For my church and community:

For our World:

Other:

DAY 14   MARK 5:25-43   SATURDAY

Meanwhile a woman who for twelve years had suffered from hemorrhage, and undergone much at the hands of many doctors, (spending all she had without obtaining any relief, but, on the contrary, growing worse), heard about Jesus, came behind in the crowd, and touched his cloak. "If I can only touch his clothes," she said, "I will get well!" At once her bleeding stopped, and she felt in herself that she was cured of her affliction. Jesus at once became aware of the power that had gone out from him, and, turning around in the crowd, he said, "Who touched my clothes?"

"You see the people pressing around you," exclaimed his disciples, "and yet you say 'Who touched me?'" But Jesus looked about to see who had done it. Then the woman, in fear and trembling, knowing what had happened to her, came and threw herself down before him, and told him the whole truth. "Daughter," he

said, "your faith has delivered you. Go, and peace be with you; be free from your affliction."

Before he had finished speaking, some people from the house of the synagogue leader came and said, "Your daughter is dead! Why should you trouble the teacher further?" But Jesus, overhearing what they were saying, said to the synagogue leader, "Do not be afraid; only have faith." And he allowed no one to accompany him, except Peter, James, and John, the brother of James. Presently they reached the leader's house, where Jesus saw a scene of confusion – people weeping and wailing incessantly. "Why this confusion and weeping?" he said on entering. "The little child is not dead; she is asleep." They began to laugh at him; but he sent them all out, and then, with the child's father and mother and his companions, went into the room where she was lying. Taking her hand, Jesus said to her, "Talitha, koum!" – which means 'little girl, I am speaking to you – Rise!' The little girl stood up at once, and began to walk about; for she was twelve years old. And, as soon as they saw it, they were overwhelmed with amazement; but Jesus repeatedly cautioned them not to let anyone know of it, and told them to give her something to eat.

REFLECTION	My Prayers for Today
Write down three words or phrases from this passage:	For myself:
1.	For my family and friends:
2.	
3.	For my church and community:
What does this say about Jesus?	For our World
	Other:

WEEK THREE

THE MESSIAH

MARK 6:1 - 7:37

DAY 15   MARK 6:1-13   SUNDAY

On leaving that place, Jesus, followed by his disciples, went to his own part of the country. When the Sabbath came, he began to teach in the synagogue; and the people, as they listened, were deeply impressed. "Where did he get this?" they said, "and what is this wisdom that has been given him? And these miracles which he is doing? Isn't he the carpenter, the son of Mary, and the brother of James, and Joses, and Judas, and Simon? And aren't his sisters, too, living here among us?" This proved a hindrance to their believing in him; at which Jesus said, "A prophet is not without honor, except in his home town, and among his own relatives, and in his own home." And he could not work any miracle there, beyond placing his hands on a few infirm persons, and curing them; and he wondered at the want of faith shown by the people.

Jesus went around the villages, one after another, teaching.

He called the Twelve to him, and began to send them out as his messengers, two and two, and gave them authority over foul spirits. He instructed them to take nothing but a staff for the journey – not even bread, or a bag, or coins in their purse; but they were to wear sandals, and not to put on a second coat. "Whenever you go to stay at a house," he said, "remain there until you leave that place; and if a place does not welcome you, or listen to you, as you go out of it shake off the dust that is on the soles of your feet, as a protest against them." So they set out, and proclaimed the need of repentance. They drove out many demons, and anointed with oil many who were infirm, and cured them.

REFLECTION

Write down three words or phrases from this passage:

1.

2.

3.

What does this say about Jesus?

My Prayers for Today

For myself:

For my family and friends:

For my church and community:

For our World:

Other:

DAY 16   MARK 6:14-29   MONDAY

Now King Herod heard of Jesus; for his name had become well known. People were saying – "John the Baptizer must have risen from the dead, and that is why these miraculous powers are active in him." Others again said – "He is Elijah," and others – "He is a prophet, like one of the great prophets." But when Herod heard of him, he said – "The man whom I beheaded – John – he must be risen!"

For Herod himself had sent and arrested John, and put him in prison, in chains, to please Herodias, the wife of his brother Philip, because Herod had married her. For John had said to Herod – "You have no right to be living with your brother's wife." So Herodias was incensed against John, and wanted to put him to death, but was unable to do so, because Herod stood in fear of John, knowing him to be an upright and holy man, and protected him. He had listened to John, but still remained much perplexed, and yet he found pleasure in listening to him.

A suitable opportunity, however, occurred when Herod, on his birthday, gave a dinner to his high officials, and his generals, and the foremost men in Galilee. When his daughter – that is, the daughter of Herodias – came in and danced, she delighted Herod and those who were dining with him. "Ask me for whatever you like," the king said to the girl, "and I will give it to you"; and he swore to her that he would give her whatever she asked him – up to half his kingdom. The girl went out, and said to her mother "What must I ask for?"

"The head of John the Baptizer," answered her mother. So she went in as quickly as possible to the king, and made her request. "I want you," she said, "to give me at once, on a dish, the head of John the Baptist." The king was much distressed; yet, because of his oath and of the guests at his table, he did not like to refuse her. He immediately dispatched one of his bodyguard, with orders to bring John's head. The man went and beheaded John in the prison, and, bringing his head on a dish, gave it to the girl, and the girl gave it to her mother.

When John's disciples heard of it, they came and took his body away, and laid it in a tomb.

REFLECTION	My Prayers for Today
Write down three words or phrases from this passage:	For myself:
1.	For my family and friends:
2.	
3.	For my church and community:
What does this say about Jesus?	For our World:
	Other:

DAY 17 MARK 6:30-44 TUESDAY

When the apostles came back to Jesus, they told him all that they had done and all that they had taught. "Come by yourselves privately to some lonely spot," he said, "and rest for a while" – for there were so many people coming and going that they had not time even to eat. So they set off privately in their boat for a lonely spot. Many people saw them going, and recognized them, and from all the towns they flocked together to the place on foot, and got there before them. On getting out of the boat, Jesus saw a great crowd, and his heart was moved at the sight of them, because they were like sheep without a shepherd; and he began to teach them many things. When it grew late, his disciples came up to him, and said, "This is a lonely spot, and it is already late. Send the people away, so that they may go to the farms and villages around and buy themselves something to eat." But Jesus answered, "It is for you to give them something to eat." "Are we to go and spend almost a year's wages on bread," they asked, "to give them to eat?"

"How many loaves have you?" he asked, "Go, and see." When they had found out, they told him, "Five, and two fish." Jesus directed them to make all the people take their seats on the green grass, in parties; and they sat down in groups – in hundreds, and in fifties. Taking the five loaves and the two fish, Jesus looked up to heaven, and said the blessing; he broke the loaves into pieces, and gave them to his disciples for them to serve out to the people, and he divided the two fish also among them all. Everyone had sufficient to eat; and they picked up enough broken pieces to fill twelve baskets, as well as some of the fish. The people who ate the bread were five thousand in number.

REFLECTION

Write down three words or phrases from this passage:

1.

2.

3.

What does this say about Jesus?

My Prayers for Today

For myself:

For my family and friends:

For my church and community:

For our World:

Other:

DAY 18   MARK 6:45-56   WEDNESDAY

Immediately afterward Jesus made his disciples get into the boat, and cross over in advance, in the direction of Bethsaida, while he himself was dismissing the crowd. After he had taken leave of the people, he went away up the hill to pray. When evening fell, the boat was out in the middle of the sea, and Jesus on the shore alone. Seeing them laboring at the oars – for the wind was against them – about three hours after midnight Jesus came towards them, walking on the water, intending to join them. But, when they saw him walking on the water, they thought it was a ghost, and cried out; for all of them saw him, and were terrified. But Jesus at once spoke to them. "Courage!" he said, "it is I; do not be afraid!" Then he got into the boat with them, and the wind dropped. The disciples were utterly amazed, for they had not understood about the loaves, their minds being slow to learn. When they had crossed over, they landed at Gennesaret, and moored the boat. But they had no sooner left her than the people, recognizing Jesus, hurried over the whole country-side, and began to carry about on mats those who were ill, wherever they heard he was. So wherever he went – to villages, or towns, or farms – they would lay their sick in the market-places, begging him to let them touch only the tassel of his cloak; and all who touched were made well.

REFLECTION

Write down three words or phrases from this passage:

1.

2.

3.

What does this say about Jesus?

My Prayers for Today

For myself:

For my family and friends:

For my church and community:

For our World:

Other:

DAY 19   MARK 7:1-13   THURSDAY

One day the Pharisees and some of the teachers of the Law who had come from Jerusalem gathered around Jesus. They had noticed that some of his disciples ate their food with their hands 'defiled,' by which they meant unwashed. (For the Pharisees, and indeed all strict Jews, will not eat without first scrupulously washing their hands, holding in this to the traditions of their ancestors. When they come from market, they will not eat without first sprinkling themselves; and there are many other customs which they have inherited and hold to, such as the ceremonial washing of cups, and jugs, and copper pans). So the Pharisees and the teachers of the Law asked Jesus this question – "How is it that your disciples do not follow the traditions of our ancestors, but eat their food with defiled hands?" His answer was, "It was well said by Isaiah when he prophesied about you hypocrites in the words – 'This is a people who honor me with their lips, while their hearts are far removed from me; but vainly do they worship me, For they teach but human precepts.' You neglect God's commandments and hold to human traditions. Wisely do you set aside God's commandments," he exclaimed, "to keep your own traditions! For while Moses said 'Honor your father and your mother,' and 'Let anyone who abuses their father or mother suffer death,' you say 'If a person says to their father or mother "Whatever of mine might have been of service to you is Corban"' (which means 'Set apart for God') – why, then you do not allow them to do anything further for their father or mother! In this way you nullify the words of God by your traditions, which you hand down; and you do many similar things."

REFLECTION

Write down three words or phrases from this passage:

1.

2.

3.

What does this say about Jesus?

My Prayers for Today

For myself:

For my family and friends:

For my church and community:

For our World:

Other:

DAY 20   MARK 7:14-23   FRIDAY

Then Jesus called the people to him again, and said, "Listen to me, all of you, and mark my words. There is nothing external to a person, which by going into them can defile them; but the things that come out of a person are the things that defile them."

When Jesus went indoors, away from the crowd, his disciples began questioning him about this saying. "What, do even you understand so little?" exclaimed Jesus. "Don't you see that there is nothing external to a person, which by going into a person, can defile them, because it does not pass into his heart, but into his stomach, and is afterward got rid of?" – in saying this Jesus pronounced all food clean. "It is what comes out from a person," he added, "that defiles them, for it is from within, out of the hearts of people, that there come evil thoughts – sexual immorality, theft, murder, adultery, greed, wickedness, deceit, indecency, envy, slander, haughtiness, folly; all these wicked things come from within, and do defile a person."

REFLECTION

Write down three words or phrases from this passage:

1.

2.

3.

What does this say about Jesus?

My Prayers for Today

For myself:

For my family and friends:

For my church and community:

For our World:

Other:

DAY 21   MARK 7:24-37   SATURDAY

On leaving that place, Jesus went to the district of Tyre and Sidon. He went into a house, and did not wish anyone to know it, but could not escape notice. For a woman, whose little daughter had a foul spirit in her, heard of him immediately, and came and threw herself at his feet – the woman was a foreigner, from Syrian Phoenicia – and she begged him to drive the demon out of her daughter. "Let the children be satisfied first," answered Jesus. "For it is not fair to take the children's food, and throw it to dogs."

"Yes, Master," she replied. "Even the dogs under the table do feed on the children's crumbs."

"For saying that," he answered, "you may go. The demon has gone out of your daughter." The woman went home, and found the child lying on her bed, and the demon gone.

On returning from the district of Tyre, Jesus went, by way of Sidon, to the Sea of Galilee, across the district of the Ten Towns. Some people brought to him a man who was deaf and almost dumb, and they begged Jesus to place his hand on him. Jesus took him aside from the crowd quietly, put his fingers into the man's ears, and touched his tongue with saliva. Then, looking up to heaven, he sighed, and said to the man, "Ephphatha!" which means 'Be opened.' The man's ears were opened, the string of his tongue was freed, and he began to talk plainly. Jesus insisted on their not telling anyone; but the more he insisted, the more perseveringly they made it known, and a profound impression was made on the people. "He has done everything well!" they exclaimed. "He makes even the deaf hear and the dumb speak!"

REFLECTION

Write down three words or phrases from this passage:

1.

2.

3.

What does this say about Jesus?

My Prayers for Today

For myself:

For my family and friends:

For my church and community:

For our World:

Other:

WEEK FOUR

THE LIFE-GIVER

MARK 8:1 - 10:52

DAY 22   MARK 8:1-10   SUNDAY

About that time, when there was again a great crowd of people who had nothing to eat, Jesus called his disciples to him, and said, "My heart is moved at the sight of all these people, for they have already been with me three days and they have nothing to eat; and if I send them away to their homes hungry, they will break down on the way; and some of them have come a long distance."

"Where will it be possible," his disciples answered, "to get sufficient bread for these people in this lonely place?"

"How many loaves have you?" he asked. "Seven," they answered. Jesus told the crowd to sit down on the ground. Then he took the seven loaves, and, after saying the thanksgiving, broke them, and gave them to his disciples to serve out; and they served them out to the crowd. They had also a few small fish; and, after he had said the blessing, he told the disciples to serve out these as well. 8The people had sufficient to eat, and they picked up seven baskets full of the broken pieces that were left. There were about four thousand people. Then Jesus dismissed them. Immediately afterward, getting into the boat with his disciples, Jesus went to the district of Dalmanutha.

REFLECTION

Write down three words or phrases from this passage:

1.

2.

3.

What does this say about Jesus?

My Prayers for Today

For myself:

For my family and friends:

For my church and community:

For our World:

Other:

DAY 23   MARK 8:11-33   MONDAY

Here the Pharisees came out, and began to argue with Jesus, asking him for some sign from the heavens, to test him. Sighing deeply, Jesus said, "Why does this generation ask for a sign? I tell you, no sign will be given it." So he left them to themselves, and, getting into the boat again, went away to the opposite shore.

Now the disciples had forgotten to take any bread with them, one loaf being all that they had in the boat. So Jesus gave them this warning. "Take care," he said, "beware of the leaven of the Pharisees and the leaven of Herod." They began talking to one another about their being short of bread; and, noticing this, Jesus said to them, "Why are you talking about your being short of bread? Don't you yet see or understand? Are your minds still so slow or comprehension? Though you have eyes, do you not see? And though you have ears, do you not hear? Don't you remember, when I broke up the five loaves for the five thousand, how many baskets of broken pieces you picked up?"

"Twelve," they said. "And when the seven for the four thousand, how many basketfuls of broken pieces did you pick up?"

"Seven," they said. "Don't you understand now?" he repeated.

They came to Bethsaida. There some people brought a blind man to Jesus, and begged him to touch him. Taking the blind man's hand, Jesus led him to the outskirts of the village, and, when he had put saliva on the man's eyes, he placed his hands on him, and asked him, "Do you see anything?" The man looked up, and said, "I see the people, for, as they walk about, they look to me like trees." Then Jesus again placed his hands on the man's eyes; and the man saw clearly, his sight was restored, and he saw everything with perfect distinctness. Jesus sent him to his home, and said, "Do not go even into the village."

Afterward Jesus and his disciples went into the villages around Caesarea Philippi; and on the way he asked his disciples this question – "Who do people say that I am?"

"John the Baptist," they answered, "but others say Elijah, while others say one of the prophets."

"But you," he asked, "who do you say that I am?" To this Peter replied, "You are the Christ." At which Jesus charged them not to say this about him to anyone. Then he began to teach them that the Son of Man must undergo much suffering, and that he must be rejected by the elders, and the chief priests, and the teachers of the Law, and be put to death, and rise again after three days. He said all this quite openly. But Peter took Jesus aside, and began to rebuke him. Jesus, however, turning around and seeing his disciples, rebuked Peter. "Out of my sight, Satan!" he exclaimed. "For you look at things, not as God does, but as people do."

Write down three words or phrases from this passage:	My Prayers for Today
	For myself:
1.	For my family and friends:
2.	For my church and community:
3.	For our World:
What does this say about Jesus?	Other:

DAY 24   MARK 8:34-9:13   TUESDAY

Calling the people and his disciples to him, Jesus said, "If anyone wishes to walk in my steps, they must renounce self, take up their cross, and follow me. For whoever wishes to save their life will lose it, and whoever, for my sake and for the sake of the good news, will lose their life will save it. What good is it to a person to gain the whole world and forfeit their life? For what could a person give that is of equal value with their life? Whoever is ashamed of me and of my teaching, in this unfaithful and wicked generation, of them will the Son of Man be ashamed, when he comes in his Father's glory with the holy angels."

"I tell you," he added, "that some of those who are standing here will not know death until they have seen the kingdom of God come in power."

Six days later, Jesus took with him Peter, James, and John, and led them up a high mountain alone by themselves. There his appearance was transformed before their eyes, and his clothes became whiter than any launderer in the whole world could bleach them. And Elijah appeared to them, in company with Moses; and they were talking with Jesus. "Rabbi," said Peter, interposing, "it is good to be here; let us make three tents, one for you, one for Moses, and one for Elijah." For he did not know what to say, because they were much afraid. Then a cloud came down and enveloped them; and from the cloud there came a voice – "This is my dearly loved son; listen to him." And suddenly, on looking around, they saw that there was now no one with them but Jesus alone.

As they were going down the mountainside, Jesus cautioned them not to relate what they had seen to anyone, until after the Son of Man had risen from the dead. They seized on these words and discussed with one another what this 'rising from the

61

dead' meant. "How is it," they asked Jesus, "that our teachers of the Law say that Elijah has to come first?"

"Elijah does indeed come first," answered Jesus, "and re-establish everything; and does not scripture speak, with regard to the Son of Man, of his undergoing much suffering and being utterly despised? But I tell you that Elijah has come, and people have treated him just as they pleased, as scripture says of him."

REFLECTION	My Prayers for Today
Write down three words or phrases from this passage:	For myself:
1.	For my family and friends:
2.	For my church and community:
3.	For our world:
What does this say about Jesus?	Other:

DAY 25   MARK 9:14-37   WEDNESDAY

When they came to the other disciples, they saw a great crowd around them, and some teachers of the Law arguing with them. But, as soon as they saw Jesus, all the people, in great astonishment, ran up and greeted him. "What are you arguing about with them?" Jesus asked. "Teacher," answered a man in the crowd, "I brought my son to see you, as he has a spirit in him that makes him mute; and, wherever it seizes him, it dashes him down; he foams at the mouth and grinds his teeth, and he is pining away. I asked your disciples to drive the spirit out, but they failed."

"Faithless generation!" exclaimed Jesus. "How long must I be with you? How long must I have patience with you? Bring the boy to me." They brought him to Jesus; but no sooner did the boy see him than the spirit threw him into convulsions; and he fell on the ground, and rolled about, foaming at the mouth. "How long has he been like this?" Jesus asked the boy's father. "From his childhood," he answered. "It has often thrown him into fire and into water to put an end to his life; but, if you can possibly do anything, take pity on us, and help us!" "Why say 'possibly'?" Jesus replied. "Everything is possible for one who has faith." The boy's father immediately cried out, "I have faith; help my want of faith!" But, when Jesus saw that a crowd was quickly collecting, he rebuked the foul spirit, "Deaf and dumb spirit, it is I who command you. Come out from him and never enter him again." With a loud cry the spirit threw the boy into repeated convulsions, and then came out from him. The boy looked like a corpse, so that most of them said that he was dead. But Jesus took his hand, and lifted him; and he stood up.

When Jesus had gone indoors, his disciples asked him privately, "Why couldn't we drive it out?"

"A spirit of this kind," he said, "can be driven out only by prayer."

Leaving that place, Jesus and his disciples went on their way through Galilee; but he did not wish anyone to know it, for he was instructing his disciples, and telling them – "The Son of Man is being betrayed into the hands of his fellow men, and they will put him to death, but, when he has been put to death, he will rise again after three days." But the disciples did not understand his meaning and were afraid to question him.

They came to Capernaum. When Jesus had gone into the house, he asked them, "What were you discussing on the way?" But they were silent; for on the way they had been arguing with one another which was the greatest. Sitting down, Jesus called the Twelve and said, "If anyone wishes to be first, he must be last of all, and servant of all." Then Jesus took a little child, and placed it in the middle of them. Taking it in his arms, he said to them, "Anyone who, for the sake of my name, welcomes even a little child like this is welcoming me, and anyone who welcomes me is welcoming not me, but him who sent me as his messenger."

Write down three words or phrases from this passage:	My Prayers for Today
1.	For myself:
2.	For my family and friends:
3.	For my church and community:
What does this say about Jesus?	For our World: Others:

DAY 26   MARK 9:38-10:16   THURSDAY

"Teacher," said John, "we saw a man driving out demons by using your name, and we tried to prevent him, because he did not follow us."

"None of you must prevent the man," answered Jesus, "for no one will use my name in working a miracle, and yet find it easy to speak evil of me. He who is not against us is for us. If anyone gives you a cup of water because you belong to Christ, I tell you, he will assuredly not lose his reward.

"And, if anyone puts temptation in the way of one of these little ones who believe in me, it would be far better for him if he had been thrown into the sea with a great millstone around his neck. If your hand causes you to sin, cut it off. It would be better for you to enter the life maimed, than to have both your hands and go into Gehenna, into the fire that cannot be put out. If your foot causes you to sin, cut it off. It would be better for you to enter the

life lame, than to have both your feet and be thrown into Gehenna. If your eye causes you to sin, tear it out. It would be better for you to enter the kingdom of God with only one eye, than to have both eyes and be thrown into Gehenna, where their worm does not die, and the fire is not put out.

For it is by fire that everyone will be salted.

Salt is good, but, if the salt should lose its saltiness, what will you use to season it?

You must have salt in yourselves, and live at peace with one another."

On leaving that place, Jesus went into the district of Judea on the other side of the Jordan. Crowds gathered about him again; and again, as usual, he began teaching them. Presently some Pharisees came up and, to test him, asked, "Has a husband the right to divorce his wife?"

"What direction did Moses give you?" replied Jesus. "Moses," they said, "permitted a man to draw up in writing a notice of separation and divorce his wife."

"It was owing to the hardness of your hearts," said Jesus, "that Moses gave you this direction; but, at the beginning of the Creation, 'God made them male and female.' 'For this reason a man will leave his father and mother, 8and the man and his wife will become one;' so that they are no longer two, but one. What God himself, then, has yoked together no one must separate."

When they were indoors, the disciples asked him again about this, and he said, "Anyone who divorces his wife and marries another woman is guilty of adultery against his wife; and, if the woman divorces her husband and marries another man, she is guilty of adultery."

Some of the people were bringing little children to Jesus, for him to touch them; but the disciples rebuked those who had brought them. When, however, Jesus saw this, he was indignant. "Let the little children come to me," he said, "do not hinder them; for it is to the childlike that the kingdom of God belongs. I tell you, unless a person receives the kingdom of God like a child, they will not enter it at all." Then he embraced the children, and, placing his hands on them, gave them his blessing.

Write down three words or phrases from this passage:	My Prayers for Today

DAY 27   MARK 10:17-34   FRIDAY

As Jesus was resuming his journey, a man came running up to him, and threw himself on his knees before him. "Good teacher," he asked, "what must I do to gain eternal life?"

"Why do you call me good?" answered Jesus. "No one is good but God. You know the commandments – 'Do not kill. Do not commit adultery. Do not steal. Do not say what is false about others. Do not cheat. Honor your father and your mother.'"

"Teacher," he replied, "I have observed all these from my childhood." Jesus looked at the man, and his heart went out to him, and he said, "There is still one thing wanting in you; go and sell all that you have, and give to the poor, and you will have wealth in heaven; then come and follow me." But the man's face clouded at these words, and he went away distressed, for he had great possessions.

Then Jesus looked around, and said to his disciples, "How hard it will be for people of wealth to enter the kingdom of God!" The disciples were amazed at his words. But Jesus said again, "My children, how hard a thing it is to enter the kingdom of God! It is easier for a camel to get through a needle's eye, than for a rich person to enter the kingdom of God."

"Then who can be saved?" they exclaimed in the greatest astonishment. Jesus looked at them, and answered, "With people it is impossible, but not with God; for everything is possible with God."

"But we," began Peter, "we left everything and have followed you."

"I tell you," said Jesus, "there is no one who has left house, or brothers, or sisters, or mother, or father, or children, or land, for my sake and for the good news, who will not receive a hundred times as much, even now in the present – houses, and brothers, and sisters, and mothers, and children, and land, though not without persecutions – and in the age that is coming, eternal life. But many who are first now will then be last, and the last will be first."

They were on the road going up to Jerusalem, with Jesus walking in front of them. The disciples were filled with awe, while those who were following behind were overwhelmed with fear. Gathering the Twelve around him once more, Jesus began to tell them what was about to happen to him. "Listen!" he said. "We are going up to Jerusalem; and there the Son of Man will be betrayed to the chief priests and the teachers of the Law, and they will condemn him to death, and they will give him up to the Gentiles, who will mock him, spit on him, and scourge him, and put him to death; and after three days he will rise again."

Write down three words or phrases from this passage:	My Prayers for Today
	For myself:
1.	
	For my family and friends:
2.	
	For my church and community:
3.	
	For our World:
What does this say about Jesus?	Other:

DAY 28   MARK 10:35-52   SATURDAY

James and John, the two sons of Zebedee, went to Jesus, and said, "Teacher, we want you to do for us whatever we ask."

"What do you want me to do for you?" he asked. "Grant us this," they answered, "to sit, one on your right, and the other on your left, when you come in glory."

"You do not know what you are asking," Jesus said to them. "Can you drink the cup that I am to drink? Or receive the baptism that I am to receive?"

"Yes," they answered, "we can."

"You will indeed drink the cup that I am to drink," Jesus said, "and receive the baptism that I am to receive, but as to a seat at my right or at my left – that is not mine to give, but it is for those for whom it has been prepared."

On hearing of this, the ten others were at first very indignant about James and John. But Jesus called the ten to him, and said, "Those who are regarded as ruling among the Gentiles lord it over them, as you know, and their great men oppress them. But among you it is not so. No, whoever wants to become great among you must be your servant, and whoever wants to take the first place among you must be the servant of all; for even the Son of Man came, not be served, but to serve, and to give his life as a ransom for many."

They came to Jericho. When Jesus was going out of the town with his disciples and a large crowd, Bartimaeus, the son of Timaeus, a blind beggar, was sitting by the roadside. Hearing that it was Jesus the Nazarene, he began to call out, "Jesus, Son of David, take pity on me." Many of the people kept telling him to be quiet; but the man continued to call out all the louder, "Son of David, take pity on me." Then Jesus stopped. "Call him," he said. So they called the blind man. "Have courage!" they exclaimed. "Get up; he is calling you." The man threw off his cloak, sprang up, and came to Jesus. "What do you want me to do for you?" said Jesus,

addressing him. "Rabboni," the blind man answered, "I want to recover my sight."

"You may go," Jesus said, "Your faith has delivered you." Immediately he recovered his sight, and began to follow Jesus along the road.

Write down three words or phrases from this passage: 1. 2. 3. What does this say about Jesus?	My Prayers for Today For myself: For my family and friends: For my church and community: For our World: Other:

WEEK FIVE

THE REBEL

MARK 11:1-14:11

DAY 29   MARK 11:1-19   SUNDAY

When they had almost reached Jerusalem, as far as Bethphage and Bethany, near the Mount of Olives, Jesus sent on two of his disciples. "Go to the village facing you," he said, "and, as soon as you get there, you will find a foal tethered, which no one has ever ridden; untie it, and bring it. 3And, if anyone says to you 'Why are you doing that?', say 'The Master wants it, and will be sure to send it back here at once.'" The two disciples went, and, finding a foal tethered outside a door in the street, they untied it. Some of the bystanders said to them, "What are you doing, untying the foal?" And the two disciples answered as Jesus had told them; and they allowed them to go. Then they brought the foal to Jesus, and, when they had laid their cloaks on it, he seated himself on it. Many of the people spread their cloaks on the road, while some strewed boughs which they had cut from the fields; and those who led the way, as well as those who followed, kept shouting, "God save him! Blessed is He who comes in the name of the Lord! Blessed is the coming kingdom of our father David! God save him from on high!"

Jesus entered Jerusalem, and went into the Temple Courts; and, after looking around at everything, as it was already late, he went out to Bethany with the Twelve.

The next day, after they had left Bethany, Jesus became hungry; and, noticing a fig-tree at a distance in leaf, he went to it to see if by any chance he could find something on it; but, on coming up to it, he found nothing but leaves, for it was not the season for figs. So, addressing the tree, he exclaimed, "May no one ever again eat of your fruit!" And his disciples heard what he said.

They came to Jerusalem. Jesus went into the Temple Courts, and began to drive out those who were buying and selling there. He overturned the tables of the money changers, and the seats of the pigeon-dealers, and would not allow anyone to carry anything across the Temple Courts. Then he began to teach. "Does not scripture say," he asked, "'My house will be called a house of prayer for all the nations'? But you have made it a den of robbers." Now the chief priests and the teachers of the Law heard this and began to look for some way of putting Jesus to death; for they were afraid of him, since all the people were greatly impressed by his teaching. As soon as evening fell, Jesus and his disciples went out of the city.

Write down three words or phrases from this passage:	**My Prayers for Today**
1.	**For myself:**
2.	**For my family and friends:**
3.	**For my church and community:**
What does this say about Jesus?	**For our World:**
	Other:

DAY 30   MARK 11:20-33   MONDAY

As they passed by early in the morning, they noticed that the fig-tree was withered up from the roots. Then Peter recalled what had occurred. "Look, Rabbi," he exclaimed, "the fig-tree which you doomed is withered up!"

"Have faith in God!" replied Jesus. "I tell you that if anyone should say to this hill 'Be lifted up and hurled into the sea!', without ever a doubt in his mind, but in the faith that what he says will be done, he would find that it would be. And therefore I say to you 'Have faith that whatever you ask for in prayer is already granted you, and you will find that it will be.'

"And, whenever you stand up to pray, forgive any grievance that you have against anyone, so that your Father who is in heaven also may forgive you your offenses." They came to Jerusalem again. While Jesus was walking about in the Temple Courts, the chief priests, the teachers of the Law, and the elders came up to him. "What authority have you to do these things?" they said. "Who gave you the authority to do them?"

"I will put one question to you," said Jesus. "Answer me that, and then I will tell you what authority I have to act as I do. It is about John's baptism. Was it of divine or human origin? Answer me that." They began arguing together. "If we say 'divine,' he will say 'Why then didn't you believe him?' Yet can we say 'human'?" They were afraid of the people, for everyone regarded John as undoubtedly a prophet. So their answer to Jesus was – "We do not know."

"Then I," replied Jesus, "refuse to tell you what authority I have to do these things."

REFLECTION

Write down three words or phrases from this passage:

1.

2.

3.

What does this say about Jesus?

My Prayers for Today

For myself:

For my family and friends:

For my church and community:

For our World:

Other:

DAY 31   MARK 12:1-12   TUESDAY

Jesus began to speak to them in parables, "A man once planted a vineyard, put a fence around it, dug a wine-press, built a tower, and then let it out to tenants and went abroad. At the proper time he sent a servant to the tenants, to receive from them a share of the produce of the grape harvest; but they seized him, and beat him, and sent him away empty-handed. A second time the owner sent a servant to them; this man, too, the tenants struck on the head, and insulted. He sent another, but him they killed; and so with many others – some they beat and some they killed. He had still one son, who was very dear to him; and him he sent to them last of all. 'They will respect my son,' he said. But those tenants said to one another 'Here is the heir! Come, let us kill him, and his inheritance will be ours.' So they seized him, and killed him, and threw his body outside the vineyard. What will the owner of the vineyard do? He will come and put the tenants to death, and he will let the vineyard to others.

"Have you never read this passage of scripture? – 'The stone which the builders despised has now itself become the corner-stone; this corner-stone has come from the Lord, and is marvelous in our eyes.'"

After this his enemies were eager to arrest him, but they were afraid of the crowd; for they saw that it was at them that he had aimed the parable. So they left him alone, and went away.

REFLECTION

Write down three words or phrases from this passage:

1.

2.

3.

What does this say about Jesus?

My Prayers for Today

For myself:

For my family and friends:

For my church and community:

For our World:

Other:

DAY 32   MARK 12:13-34   WEDNESDAY

Afterward they sent to Jesus some of the Pharisees and Herodians, to set a trap for him in the course of conversation. These men came to him and said, "Teacher, we know that you are an honest man, and are not afraid of anyone, for you pay no regard to a person's position, but teach the way of God honestly; are we right in paying taxes to the Emperor, or not? Should we pay, or should we not pay?" Knowing their hypocrisy, Jesus said to them, "Why are you testing me? Bring me a coin to look at." And, when they had brought it, he asked, "Whose head and title are these?"

"The Emperor's," they said; and Jesus replied, "Pay to the Emperor what belongs to the Emperor, and to God what belongs to God." And they wondered at him.

Next came some Sadducees – the men who maintain that there is no resurrection. Their question was this – "Teacher, in our scriptures Moses decreed that, should a man's brother die, leaving a widow but no child, the man should take the widow as his wife, and raise up a family for his brother. There were once seven brothers. The eldest married, but died and left no family; and the second married his widow, and died without family; and so did the third. All the seven died and left no family. The woman herself died last of all. At the resurrection whose wife will she be, all seven brothers having had her as their wife?"

"Is not the reason of your mistake," answered Jesus, "your ignorance of the scriptures and of the power of God? When people rise from the dead, there is no marrying or being married; but they are as angels in heaven.

"As to the dead, and the fact that they rise, have you never read in the book of Moses, in the passage about the Bush, how God spoke to him saying –

'I am the God of Abraham, and the God of Isaac, and the God of Jacob'? He is not God of dead people, but of living. You are greatly mistaken."

Then came up one of the teachers of the Law who had heard their discussions. Knowing that Jesus had answered them wisely, he asked him this question, "Which commandment is the most important of all?"

"The most important," answered Jesus, "is – 'Hear, Israel; the Lord our God is the one Lord; and you must love the Lord your God with all your heart, and with all your soul, and with all your mind, and with all your strength.' The second is this – 'You must love your neighbor as you love yourself.' There is no commandment greater than these."

"Wisely answered, teacher!" exclaimed the teacher of the Law. "It is true, as you say, that there is one God, and that there is no other besides him; and to love him with all one's heart, and with all one's understanding, and with all one's strength, and to love one's neighbor as one loves oneself is far beyond all burnt offerings and sacrifices." Seeing that he had answered with discernment, Jesus said to him, "You are not far from the kingdom of God."

After that no one ventured to question him further.

Write down three words or phrases from this passage:	My Prayers for Today

DAY 33   MARK 12:35-13:2   THURSDAY

While Jesus was teaching in the Temple Courts, he asked, "How is it that the teachers of the Law say that the Christ is to be David's son? David said himself, speaking under the inspiration of the Holy Spirit – 'The Lord said to my lord: Sit at my right hand, until I put your enemies beneath your feet.' David himself calls him 'lord,' how comes it, then, that he is to be his son?"

The mass of the people listened to Jesus with delight. In the course of his teaching, Jesus said, "See that you are on your guard against the teachers of the Law, who delight to walk about in long robes, and to be greeted in the streets with respect, and to have the best seats in the synagogues, and places of honor at dinner. They are the men who rob widows of their homes, and make a pretense of saying long prayers. Their sentence will be all the heavier."

Then Jesus sat down opposite the chests for the Temple offerings, and watched how the people put money into them. Many rich people were putting in large sums; but one poor widow came and put in two small coins, worth very little. Then, calling his disciples to him, Jesus said, "I tell you that this poor widow has put in more than all the others who were putting money into the chests; for everyone else put in something from what he had to spare, while she, in her need, put in all she had – everything that she had to live on."

As Jesus was walking out of the Temple Courts, one of his disciples said to him, "Teacher, look what fine stones and buildings these are!"

"Do you see these great buildings?" asked Jesus. "Not a single stone will be left here on another, which will not be thrown down."

REFLECTION

Write down three words or phrases from this passage:

1.

2.

3.

What does this say about Jesus?

My Prayers for Today

For myself:

For my family and friends:

For my church and community:

For our World:

Other:

DAY 34   MARK 13:3-27   FRIDAY

When Jesus had sat down on the Mount of Olives, facing the Temple, Peter, James, John and Andrew questioned him privately, "Tell us when this will be, and what will be the sign when all this is drawing to its close."

Then Jesus began, "See that no one leads you astray. Many will take my name, and come saying 'I am He', and will lead many astray.

"And, when you hear of wars and rumors of wars, do not be alarmed; such things must occur; but the end is not yet. For nation will rise against nation, and kingdom against kingdom; there will be earthquakes in various places; there will be famines. This will be but the beginning of the birth-pangs.

"See to yourselves! They will betray you to courts of law; and you will be taken to synagogues and beaten; and you will be brought up before governors and kings for my sake, so that you can bear witness before them. But the good news must first be proclaimed to every nation. Whenever they betray you and hand you over for trial, do not be anxious beforehand as to what you will say, but say whatever is given you at the moment; for it will not be you who speak, but the Holy Spirit. Brother will betray brother to death, and the father his child; and children will turn against their parents, and cause them to be put to death; and you will be hated by everyone because of me. Yet the person who endures to the end will be saved.

"As soon, however, as you see 'the Foul Desecration' standing where it ought not" (the reader must consider what this means) "then those of you who are in Judea must take refuge in the mountains; and a person on the house-top must not go down, or go in to get anything out of their house: nor must one who is on their farm turn back to get their cloak. And alas for pregnant women, and for those who are nursing infants in those days! Pray, too, that this may not occur in winter. For those days will be a time of distress, the like of which has not occurred from the beginning of God's creation until now – and never will again. And, had not the Lord put a limit to those days, not a single soul would escape; but, for the sake of God's own chosen people, he did limit them.

"And at that time if anyone should say to you 'Look, here is the Christ!' 'Look, there he is!', do not believe it; for false Christs and false prophets will arise, and display signs and marvels, to lead astray, were it possible, even God's people. But see that you are on your guard! I have told you all this beforehand.

"In those days, after that time of distress, the sun will be darkened, the moon will not give her light, the stars will be falling from the heavens, and the forces that are in the heavens will be convulsed. Then will be seen the Son of Man coming in clouds with great power and glory; and then he will send the angels, and gather his people from the four winds, from one end of the world to the other.

Write down three words or phrases from this passage:	My Prayers for Today

DAY 35   MARK 13:38-14:11 SATURDAY

"Learn the lesson taught by the fig-tree. As soon as its branches are full of sap, and it is bursting into leaf, you know that summer is near. And so may you, as soon as you see these things happening, know that he is at your doors. I tell you that even the present generation will not pass away, until all these things have taken place. The heavens and the earth will pass away, but my words will not pass away.

"But about that day, or the hour, no one knows – not even the angels in heaven, not even the Son – but only the Father.

"See that you are on the watch; for you do not know when the time will be. It is like a man going on a journey, who leaves his home, puts his servants in charge – each having their special duty – and orders the porter to watch. Therefore watch, for you cannot be sure when the Master of the house is coming – whether in the evening, at midnight, at daybreak, or in the morning – otherwise he might come suddenly and find you asleep. And what I say to you I say to all – Watch!"

It was now two days before the Festival of the Passover and the unleavened bread. The chief priests and the teachers of the Law were looking for an opportunity to arrest Jesus by stealth, and to put him to death; for they said, "Not during the Festival, or the people may riot."

When Jesus was still at Bethany, in the house of Simon the leper, while he was sitting at the table, a woman came with an alabaster jar of choice spikenard perfume of great value. She broke the jar, and poured the perfume on his head. Some of those who were present said to one another indignantly, "Why has the perfume been wasted like this? This perfume could have been sold for more than a year's wages, and the money given to the poor."

"Leave her alone," said Jesus, as they began to find fault with her, "why are you troubling her? This is a beautiful deed that she has done for me. You always have the poor with you, and whenever you wish you can do good to them; but you will not always have me. She has done what she could; she has perfumed my body beforehand for my burial. And I tell you, wherever, in the whole world, the good news is proclaimed, what this woman has done will be told in memory of her."

After this, Judas Iscariot, one of the Twelve, went to the chief priests, to betray Jesus to them. They were glad to hear what he said, and promised to pay him. So he began looking for a good opportunity to betray Jesus.

REFLECTION	My Prayers for Today
Write down three words or phrases from this passage:	For myself:
1.	For my family and friends:
2.	For my church and community:
3.	For our world:
What does this say about Jesus?	Other:

WEEK SIX

THE SAVIOR

MARK 14:12-15:47

DAY 36   MARK 14:12-25   SUNDAY

On the first day of the Festival of the unleavened bread, when it was customary to kill the Passover lambs, his disciples said to Jesus, "Where do you wish us to go and make preparations for your eating the Passover?" Jesus sent forward two of his disciples and said to them, "Go into the city, and there a man carrying a pitcher of water will meet you; follow him; and, wherever he goes in, say to the owner of the house 'The teacher says – Where is my room where I am to eat the Passover with my disciples?' He will himself show you a large upstairs room, set out ready; and there make preparations for us." So the disciples set out and went into the city, and found everything just as Jesus had told them; and they prepared the Passover.

In the evening he went there with the Twelve, and when they had taken their places and were eating, Jesus said, "I tell you that one of you is going to betray me – one who is eating with me." They were grieved at this, and began to say to him, one after another, "Can it be I?"

"It is one of you Twelve," said Jesus, "the one who is dipping his bread beside me into the dish. True, the Son of Man must go, as scripture says of him, yet alas for that man by whom the Son of Man is being betrayed! For that man it would be better never to have been born!"

While they were eating, Jesus took some bread, and, after saying the blessing, broke it, and gave it to them, and said, "Take it; this is my body." Then he took a cup, and, after saying the thanksgiving, gave it to them, and they all drank from it. "This is my covenant-blood," he said, "which is poured out on behalf of many. I tell you that I will never again drink of the juice of the grape, until that day when I will drink it new in the kingdom of God."

REFLECTION

Write down three words or phrases from this passage:

1.

2.

3.

What does this say about Jesus?

My Prayers for Today

For myself:

For my family and friends:

For my church and community:

For our World:

Other:

DAY 37   MARK 14:26-42   MONDAY

They then sang a hymn, and went out up the Mount of Olives, presently Jesus said to them, "All of you will fall away; for scripture says – 'I will strike down the shepherd, and the sheep will be scattered.' Yet, after I have risen, I will go before you into Galilee."

"Even if everyone else falls away," said Peter, "I will not."

"I tell you," answered Jesus, "that you yourself today – yes, this very night – before the cock crows twice, will disown me three times." But Peter vehemently protested, "Even if I must die with you, I will never disown you!" And they all said the same.

Presently they came to a garden known as Gethsemane, and Jesus said to his disciples "Sit down here while I pray." He took with him Peter, James, and John; and began to show signs of great dismay and deep distress of mind. "I am sad at heart," he said, "sad even to death; wait here,

and watch." Going on a little further, he threw himself on the ground, and began to pray that, if it were possible, he might be spared that hour. "Abba, Father," he said, "all things are possible to you; take away this cup from me; yet, not what I will, but what you will."

Then he came and found the three apostles asleep. "Simon," he said to Peter, "are you asleep? Couldn't you watch for one hour? Watch and pray," he said to them all, "so that you may not fall into temptation. True, the spirit is willing, but the flesh is weak." Again he went away, and prayed in the same words; and coming back again he found them asleep, for their eyes were heavy; and they did not know what to say to him.

A third time he came, and said to them, "Sleep on now, and rest yourselves. Enough! My time has come. Look, the Son of Man is being betrayed into the hands of wicked people. Up, and let us be going. Look!

My betrayer is close at hand."

REFLECTION

Write down three words or phrases from this passage:

1.

2.

3.

What does this say about Jesus?

My Prayers for Today

For myself:

For my family and friends:

For my church and community:

For our World:

Other:

DAY 38   MARK 14:43-65   TUESDAY

And just then, while he was still speaking, Judas, who was one of the Twelve, came up; and with him a crowd of people, with swords and clubs, sent by the chief priests, the teachers of the Law, and the elders. Now the betrayer had arranged a signal with them. "The man whom I kiss," he had said, "will be the one; arrest him and take him away safely." As soon as Judas came, he went up to Jesus at once, and said, "Rabbi!" and kissed him. Then the men seized Jesus, and arrested him.

One of those who were standing by drew his sword, and struck at the high priest's servant, and cut off his ear. But Jesus spoke up, and said to the men, "Have you come out, as if after a robber, with swords and clubs, to take me? I have been among you day after day in the Temple Courts teaching, and yet you did not arrest me; but this is in fulfillment of the scriptures." And all the apostles deserted him and fled. One young man did indeed follow him, wrapped only in a linen sheet. They tried to arrest him; but he left the sheet in their hands, and fled naked.

Then they took Jesus to the high priest; and all the chief priests, elders, and the teachers of the Law assembled. Peter, who had followed Jesus at a distance into the courtyard of the high priest, was sitting there among the police officers, warming himself at the blaze of the fire.

Meanwhile the chief priest and the whole of the High Council were trying to get such evidence against Jesus as would warrant his being put to death, but they could not find any; for, though there were many who gave false evidence against him, yet their evidence did not agree. Presently some men stood up, and gave this false evidence against him – "We ourselves heard him say 'I will destroy this Temple made with hands, and in three days build another made without hands.'" Yet not even on that point did their evidence agree.

Then the high priest stood forward, and questioned Jesus. "Have you no answer to make?" he asked. "What is this evidence which these men are giving against you?" But Jesus remained silent, and made no answer.

A second time the high priest questioned him. "Are you," he asked, "the Christ, the Son of the Blessed One?"

"I am," replied Jesus, "and you will all see the Son of Man sitting on the right hand of the Almighty, and coming in the clouds of heaven." At this the high priest tore his vestments. "Why do we want any more witnesses?" he exclaimed. "You heard his blasphemy? What is your verdict?" They all condemned him, declaring that he deserved death.

Some of those present began to spit at him, and to blindfold his eyes, and strike him, saying, as they did so, "Now play the prophet!" and even the temple guards received him with blows.

Write down three words or phrases from this passage:	My Prayers for Today

DAY 39   MARK 14:66-72   WEDNESDAY

While Peter was in the courtyard down below, one of the high priest's maidservants came up; and, seeing Peter warming himself, she looked closely at him, and exclaimed, "Why, you were with Jesus, the Nazarene!" But Peter denied it. "I do not know or understand what you mean," he replied. Then he went out into the porch; and there the maidservant, on seeing him, began to say again to the bystanders, "This is one of them!" But Peter again denied it.

Soon afterward the bystanders again said to him, "You certainly are one of them; why you are a Galilean!" But he said to them, "I swear that I do not know the man you are talking about! May God punish me if I am lying!" At that moment, for the second time, a cock crowed; and Peter remembered the words that Jesus had said to him – 'Before a cock has crowed twice, you will disown me three times'; and, as he thought of it, he began to weep.

REFLECTION

Write down three words or phrases from this passage:

1.

2.

3.

What does this say about Jesus?

My Prayers for Today

For myself:

For my family and friends:

For my church and community:

For our World:

Other:

DAY 40   MARK 15:1-15   THURSDAY

As soon as it was daylight, the chief priests, after holding a consultation with elders and teachers of the Law – that is to say, the whole High Council – put Jesus in chains, and took him away, and gave him up to Pilate. "Are you the king of the Jews?" asked Pilate. "It is true," replied Jesus. Then the chief priests brought a number of charges against him. So Pilate questioned Jesus again. "Have you no reply to make?" he asked. "Listen, how many charges they are bringing against you." But Jesus still made no reply whatever; at which Pilate was astonished.

Now, at the feast, Pilate used to grant the people the release of any one prisoner whom they might ask for. A man called Barabbas was in prison, with the rioters who had committed murder during a riot. So, when the crowd went up and began to ask Pilate to follow his usual custom, he answered, "Do you want me to release the 'king of the Jews' for you?" For he was aware that it was out of jealousy that the chief priests had given Jesus up to him. But the chief priests incited the crowd to get Barabbas released instead. Pilate, however, spoke to them again, "What should I do then with the man whom you call the 'king of the Jews'?" Again they shouted, "Crucify him!"

"Why, what harm has he done?" Pilate kept saying to them. But they shouted furiously, "Crucify him!" And Pilate, wishing to satisfy the crowd, released Barabbas to them, and, after scourging Jesus, gave him up to be crucified.

REFLECTION

Write down three words or phrases from this passage:

1.

2.

3.

What does this say about Jesus?

My Prayers for Today

For myself:

For my family and friends:

For my church and community:

For our World:

Other:

DAY 41   MARK 15:16-39   FRIDAY

The soldiers then took Jesus away into the courtyard – that is the Government house – and they called the whole garrison together. They dressed him in a purple robe, and, having twisted a crown of thorns, put it on him, and then began to salute him. "Long life to you, king of the Jews!" they said. And they kept striking him on the head with a rod, spitting at him, and bowing to the ground before him – going down on their knees; and, when they had left off mocking him, they took off the purple robe, and put his own clothes on him.

They led Jesus out to crucify him; and they compelled a passer-by, Simon from Cyrene, who was on his way in from the country, the father of Alexander and Rufus, to go with them to carry his cross.

They brought Jesus to the place which was known as Golgotha – a name which means 'place of a Skull.' There they offered him drugged wine; but Jesus refused it. Then they crucified him, and divided his clothes among them, casting lots for them, to settle what each should take.

It was nine in the morning when they crucified him. The words of the charge against him, written up over his head, read – 'THE KING OF THE JEWS.' And with him they crucified two robbers, one on the right, and the other on the left.

The passers-by railed at him, shaking their heads, as they said, "Ah! You who would destroy the Temple and build one in three days, come down from the cross and save yourself!" In the same way the chief priests, with the teachers of the Law, said to one another in mockery, "He saved others, but he cannot save himself! Let the Christ, the 'king of Israel,' come down from the cross now so that we can see it and believe." Even the men who had been crucified with Jesus insulted him.

At midday, a darkness came over the whole country, lasting until three in the afternoon. And, at three, Jesus called out loudly, "Eloi, Eloi, lama sabacthani?" which means 'My God, my God, why have you forsaken me?' Some of those standing around heard this, and said, "Listen! He is calling for Elijah!" And a man ran, and, soaking a sponge in common wine, put it on the end of a rod, and offered it to him to drink, saying as he did so, "Wait and let us see if Elijah is coming to take him down." But Jesus, giving a loud cry, breathed his last. The Temple curtain was torn in two from top to bottom. The Roman officer, who was standing facing Jesus, on seeing the way in which he breathed his last, exclaimed, "This man must indeed have been God's son!"

REFLECTION	My Prayers for Today
Write down three words or phrases from this passage:	For myself:
1.	For my family and friends:
2.	For my church and community:
3.	For our world:
What does this say about Jesus?	Other:

DAY 42   MARK 15:40-47   SATURDAY

There were some women also watching from a distance, among them being Mary of Magdala, Mary the mother of James the Little and of Joseph, and Salome – all of whom used to accompany Jesus when he was in Galilee, and give him support – besides many other women who had come up with him to Jerusalem.

The evening had already fallen, when, as it was the Preparation day – the day before the Sabbath – Joseph from Ramah, a councilor of good position, who was himself living in expectation of the kingdom of God, came and ventured to go in to see Pilate, and to ask for the body of Jesus. But Pilate was surprised to hear that he had already died. So he sent for the officer, and asked if he were already dead; and, on learning from the officer that it was so, he gave the corpse to Joseph. Joseph, having bought a linen sheet, took Jesus down, and wound the sheet around him, and laid him in a tomb which had been cut out of the rock; and then rolled a stone up against the entrance of the tomb. Mary of Magdala and Mary, the mother of Joseph, were watching to see where he was laid.

REFLECTION

Write down three words or phrases from this passage:

1.

2.

3.

What does this say about Jesus?

My Prayers for Today

For myself:

For my family and friends:

For my church and community:

For our World:

Other:

WEEK SEVEN

THE WAY

MARK 16:1-20

JOHN 20:19-21:25

LUKE 24:13-53

ACTS 1:6-11

DAY 43   MARK 16:1-20   SUNDAY

When the Sabbath was over, Mary of Magdala, Mary the mother of James, and Salome bought some spices, so that they might go and anoint the body of Jesus. Very early on the first day of the week they went to the tomb, after sunrise. They were saying to one another, "Who will roll away the stone for us from the entrance of the tomb?" But, on looking up, they saw that the stone had already been rolled back; it was a very large one. Going into the tomb, they saw a young man sitting on their right, in a white robe, and they were dismayed; but he said to them, "Do not be dismayed; you are looking for Jesus, the Nazarene, who has been crucified; he has risen, he is not here! Look! Here is the place where they laid him. But go, and say to his disciples and to Peter 'He is going before you into Galilee; there you will see him, as he told you.'" They went out, and fled from the tomb, for they were trembling and bewildered;

and they did not say a word to anyone, for they were frightened.

A late appendix

(Inserted in some manuscripts from an ancient source)

After his rising again, early on the first day of the week, Jesus appeared first of all to Mary of Magdala, from whom he had driven out seven demons. She went and told the news to those who had been with him and who were now in sorrow and tears; yet even they, when they heard that he was alive and had been seen by her, did not believe it. Afterward, altered in appearance, he made himself known to two of them, as they were walking, on their way into the country. They also went and told the rest, but they did not believe even them. Later on, he made himself known to the Eleven themselves as they were at a meal, and reproached them with their want of faith and their stubbornness, because they did not believe those who had seen him after he had risen from the dead. Then he said to them, "Go into all the world, and proclaim the good news to all creation. He who believes and is baptized will be saved; but he who refuses to believe will be condemned. Moreover these signs will attend those who believe. In my name they will drive out demons; they will speak in new languages; they will take up snakes in their hands; and, if they drink any poison, it will not hurt them; they will place their hands on sick people and they will recover." So the Lord Jesus, after he had spoken to them, was taken up into heaven, and sat at the right hand of God. But they set out, and made the proclamation everywhere, the Lord working with them, and confirming the message by the signs which attended it.

Another appendix

But all that had been revealed to them they reported briefly to Peter and his companions. Afterward Jesus himself sent them out, from east to west, the sacred and imperishable proclamation of eternal salvation.

Write down three words or phrases from this passage: 1. 2. 3. What does this say about Jesus?	My Prayers for Today For myself: For my family and friends: For my church and community: For our world: Other:

DAY 44 JOHN 20:19-23 MONDAY

In the evening of the same day – the first day of the week – after the doors of the room, in which the disciples were, had been shut because they were afraid of the religious authorities, Jesus came and stood among them and said, "Peace be with you"; after which he showed them his hands and his side. The disciples were filled with joy when they saw the Master. Again Jesus said to them, "Peace be with you. As the Father has sent me as his messenger, so I am sending you." After saying this, he breathed on them, and said, "Receive the Holy Spirit; if you remit anyone's sins, they have been remitted; and, if you retain them, they have been retained."

REFLECTION

Write down three words or phrases from this passage:

1.

2.

3.

What does this say about Jesus?

My Prayers for Today

For myself:

For my family and friends:

For my church and community:

For our World:

Other:

DAY 45   JOHN 20:24-30   TUESDAY

But Thomas, one of the Twelve, called 'The Twin,' was not with them when Jesus came; so the rest of the disciples said to him, "We have seen the Master!"

"Unless I see the marks of the nails in his hands," he exclaimed, "and put my finger into the marks, and put my hand into his side, I will not believe it." A week later the disciples were again in the house, and Thomas with them. After the doors had been shut, Jesus came and stood among them, and said, "Peace be with you." Then he said to Thomas, "Place your finger here, and look at my hands; and place your hand here, and put it into my side; and do not refuse to believe, but believe." And Thomas exclaimed, "My Master, and my God!"

"Is it because you have seen me that you have believed?" said Jesus. "Blessed are they who have not seen, and yet have believed!"

There were many other signs of his mission that Jesus gave in presence of the disciples, which are not recorded in this book; but these have been recorded so that you may believe that Jesus is the Christ, the Son of God – and that, through your belief in his name, you may have life.

REFLECTION

Write down three words or phrases from this passage:

1.

2.

3.

What does this say about Jesus?

My Prayers for Today

For myself:

For my family and friends:

For my church and community:

For our World:

Other:

DAY 46   JOHN 21:1-14   WEDNESDAY

Later on, Jesus showed himself again to the disciples by the Sea of Tiberias. It was in this way, – Simon Peter, Thomas, who was called 'The Twin,' Nathanael of Cana in Galilee, Zebedee's sons, and two other disciples of Jesus, were together, when Simon Peter said, "I am going fishing."

"We will come with you," said the others. They went out and got into the boat, but caught nothing that night. Just as day was breaking, Jesus came and stood on the beach; but the disciples did not know that it was he. "My children," he said, "have you anything to eat?"

"No," they answered. "Cast your net to the right of the boat," he said, "and you will find fish." So they cast the net, and now they could not haul it in because of the quantity of fish. The disciple whom Jesus loved said to Peter, "It is the Master!" When Simon Peter heard that it was the Master, he fastened his coat around him (for he had taken it off), and threw himself into the sea. But the rest of the disciples came in the boat (for they were only about a hundred yards from shore), dragging the net full of fish. When they had come ashore, they found a charcoal fire ready, with some fish already on it, and some bread as well. "Bring some of the fish which you have just caught," said Jesus. So Simon Peter got into the boat and hauled the net ashore full of large fish, a hundred and fifty-three of them; and yet, although there were so many, the net had not been torn. "Come and have breakfast.", Jesus said. None of the disciples dared ask him who he was, because they knew it was the Master. Jesus went and took the bread and gave it to them, and the fish too. This was the third time that Jesus showed himself to the disciples after he had risen from the dead.

REFLECTION

Write down three words or phrases from this passage:

1.

2.

3.

What does this say about Jesus?

My Prayers for Today

For myself:

For my family and friends:

For my church and community:

For our World:

Other:

DAY 47   JOHN 21:15-25   THURSDAY

When breakfast was over, Jesus said to Simon Peter, "Simon, son of John, do you love me more than the others?"

"Yes, Master," he answered, "you know that I am your friend."

"Feed my lambs," said Jesus. Then, a second time, Jesus asked, "Simon, son of John, do you love me?"

"Yes, Master," he answered, "you know that I am your friend."

"Tend my sheep," said Jesus. The third time, Jesus said to him, "Simon, son of John, are you my friend?" Peter was hurt at his third question being 'Are you my friend?'; and exclaimed, "Master, you know everything! You can tell that I am your friend."

"Feed my sheep," said Jesus. "In truth I tell you," he continued, "when you were young, you used to put on your own clothes, and walk wherever you wished; but, when you have grown old, you will have to stretch out your hands, while someone else puts on your clothes, and takes you where you do not wish." Jesus said this to show the death by which Peter was to honor God, and then he added, "Follow me." Peter turned around, and saw the disciple whom Jesus loved following – the one who at the supper leant back on the Master's shoulder, and asked him who it was who would betray him. Seeing him, Peter said to Jesus, "Master, what about this man?"

"If it is my will that he should wait until I come," answered Jesus, "what has that to do with you? Follow me yourself." So the report spread among his followers that that disciple was not to die; yet Jesus did not say that he was not to die, but said "If it is my will that he should wait until I come, what has that to do with you?"

It is this disciple who states these things, and who recorded them; and we know that his statement is true.

There are many other things which Jesus did; but, if every one of them were to be recorded in detail, I suppose that even the world itself would not hold the books that would be written.

REFLECTION

Write down three words or phrases from this passage:

1.

2.

3.

What does this say about Jesus?

My Prayers for Today

For myself:

For my family and friends:

For my church and community:

For our World:

Other:

DAY 48   LUKE 24:13-24   FRIDAY

It happened that very day that two of the disciples were going to a village called Emmaus, which was about seven miles from Jerusalem, talking together, as they went, about all that had just taken place. While they were talking about these things and discussing them, Jesus himself came up and went on their way with them; but their eyes were blinded so that they could not recognize him. "What is this that you are saying to each other as you walk along?" Jesus asked. They stopped, with sad looks on their faces, and then one of them, whose name was Cleopas, said to Jesus, "Are you staying by yourself at Jerusalem, that you have not heard of the things that have happened there within the last few days?"

"What things do you mean?" asked Jesus. "Why, about Jesus of Nazareth," they answered, "who, in the eyes of God and all the people, was a prophet, whose power was felt in both his words and actions; and how the chief priests and our leading men gave him up to be sentenced to death, and afterward crucified him. But we were hoping that he was the Destined Deliverer of Israel; yes, and besides all this, it is now three days since these things occurred. And what is more, some of the women among us have greatly astonished us. They went to the tomb at daybreak And, not finding the body of Jesus there, came and told us that they had seen a vision of angels who told them that he was alive. So some of our number went to the tomb and found everything just as the women had said, but they did not see Jesus."

REFLECTION

Write down three words or phrases from this passage:

1.

2.

3.

What does this say about Jesus?

My Prayers for Today

For myself:

For my family and friends:

For my church and community:

For our World:

Other:

DAY 49   LUKE 24:25-44   SATURDAY

Then Jesus said to them, "Foolish men, slow to accept all that the prophets have said! Was not the Christ bound to undergo this suffering before entering into his glory?" Then, beginning with Moses and all the prophets, he explained to them all through the scriptures the passages that referred to himself. When they got near the village to which they were walking, Jesus appeared to be going further; but they pressed him not to do so. "Stay with us," they said, "for it is getting towards evening, and the sun in already low." So Jesus went in to stay with them. After he had taken his place at the table with them, he took the bread and said the blessing, and broke it, and gave it to them. Then their eyes were opened and they recognized him; but he disappeared from their sight. "How our hearts glowed," the disciples said to each other, "while he was talking to us on the road, and when he explained the scriptures to us!"

Then they immediately got up and returned to Jerusalem, where they found the Eleven and their companions all together, who told them that the Master had really risen, and had appeared to Simon. So they also related what had happened during their walk, and how they had recognized Jesus at the breaking of the bread. While they were still talking about these things, Jesus himself stood among them. In their terror and alarm they thought they saw a ghost, but Jesus said to them, "Why are you so startled? And why do doubts arise in your minds? Look at my hands and my feet, and you will know that it is I. Feel me, and look at me, for a ghost has not flesh and bones, as you see that I have. While they were still unable to believe it all, overcome with joy, and were wondering if it were true, Jesus said to them, "Have you anything here

117

to eat?" They handed him a piece of broiled fish, and he took it and ate it before their eyes. "This is what I told you," he said, "when I was still with you – that everything that had been written about me in the Law of Moses, the prophets, and the Psalms, must be fulfilled."

REFLECTION

Write down three words or phrases from this passage:

1.

2.

3.

What does this say about Jesus?

My Prayers for Today

For myself:

For my family and friends:

For my church and community:

For our World:

Other:

DAY 50   LUKE 24:45-53   SUNDAY

Then he enabled them to understand the meaning of the scriptures, saying to them, "Scripture says that the Christ will suffer, and that he will rise again from the dead on the third day, and that repentance for forgiveness of sins will be proclaimed on his authority to all the nations – beginning at Jerusalem. You yourselves are to be witnesses to all this. And now I am myself about to send you that which my Father has promised. But you must remain in the city until you have been invested with power from above."

After this, Jesus led them out as far as Bethany, and there raised his hands and blessed them. As he was in the act of blessing them, he left them. They returned to Jerusalem full of joy; and they were constantly in the Temple Courts, blessing God.

ACTS 1:6-11

So, when the apostles had met together, they asked Jesus this question – "Master, is this the time when you intend to re-establish the kingdom for Israel?" His answer was, "It is not for you to know times or hours, for the Father has reserved these for his own decision; but you will receive power, when the Holy Spirit will have descended on you, and will be witnesses for me not only in Jerusalem, but throughout Judea and Samaria, and to the ends of the earth."

No sooner had Jesus said this than he was caught up before their eyes, and a cloud received him from their sight. While they were still gazing up into the heavens, as he went, suddenly two men, clothed in white, stood beside them, and said, "People of Galilee, why are you standing here looking up into the heavens? This same Jesus, who has been taken from you into the heavens, will come in the same way in which you have seen him go into the heavens.

REFLECTION

Write down three words or phrases from this passage:

1.

2.

3.

What does this say about Jesus?

My Prayers for Today

For myself:

For my family and friends:

For my church and community:

For our World :   **Other:**

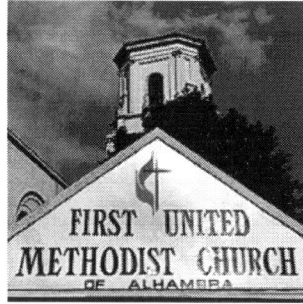

JOIN US FOR OUR ONLINE WORSHIP VIDEOS
AT FIRST ALHAMBRA METHODIST YOUTUBE

1. Go online to www.youtube.com
2. In search, type: First Alhambra Methodist
3. View the current video

First United Methodist Church of Alhambra

(阿罕布拉市第一聯合衛理公會)

9 N. Almansor St., Alhambra, CA 91801

firstumcalhambra@sbcglobal.net

625-289-4258

English Ministry: Pastor Craig Kennet Miller
                           revcraigmiller@gmail.com

Chinese Ministry: Pastor Tom Tseng(曾慶華牧師)
                           pastortom89@gmail.com

Facebook Live Worship in Mandarin – 11:00 am Sundays

https://www.facebook.com/fumcalhambra

Made in the USA
Las Vegas, NV
06 February 2021